Hodder Cambridge Primary
English
Activity Book A

Foundation Stage

Ruth Price

Acknowledgements

Every effort has been made to trace all copyright holders, but if any have been inadvertently overlooked the Publishers will be pleased to make the necessary arrangements at the first opportunity.

Hachette UK's policy is to use papers that are natural, renewable and recyclable products and made from wood grown in well-managed forests and other controlled sources. The logging and manufacturing processes are expected to conform to the environmental regulations of the country of origin.

Orders: please contact Hachette UK Distribution, Hely Hutchinson Centre, Milton Road, Didcot, Oxfordshire, OX11 7HH. Telephone: +44 (0)1235 827827. Email: education@hachette.co.uk. Lines are open from 9.00–5.00, Monday to Saturday, with a 24-hour message answering service. You can also order through our website www.hoddereducation.com

© Ruth Price 2019

Published by Hodder Education

An Hachette UK Company

Carmelite House, 50 Victoria Embankment, London EC4Y 0DZ

Impression number   5 4

Year   2023 2022

All rights reserved. Apart from any use permitted under UK copyright law, no part of this publication may be reproduced or transmitted in any form or by any means, electronic or mechanical, including photocopying and recording, or held within any information storage and retrieval system, without permission in writing from the publisher or under licence from the Copyright Licensing Agency Limited. Further details of such licences (for reprographic reproduction) may be obtained from the Copyright Licensing Agency Limited, www.cla.co.uk

Cover illustrations by Steve Evans

Illustrations by Vian Oelofsen

Typeset in FS Albert Regular 17/19 pt by Lizette Watkiss

Printed in the United Kingdom

A catalogue record for this title is available from the British Library

978 1 5104 5724 9

MIX
Paper | Supporting responsible forestry
FSC™ C104740

The authorised representative in the EEA is Hachette Ireland, 8 Castlecourt Centre, Dublin 15, D15 XTP3, Ireland (email: info@hbgi.ie)

Contents

Understanding, listening and speaking
Talking about things we need ... 4
Questions and answers ... 6
Matching and describing things we can do ... 8

Exploring words
Word families: things I can do ... 10
Repeating word patterns ... 14
Joining sentences with *and* ... 16

Tuning in to sounds and rhyme
Sounds all around us ... 18
Make the sound! ... 20
Rhyming words ... 22

Letters and sounds 1
Matching letter sounds to letter shapes ... 26
Reading words ... 27
Writing letters ... 28

Reading real-life stories
Story characters ... 30
Story settings ... 32
Story events ... 34

Writing
Writing patterns ... 38
Matching letter shapes ... 40
Matching lower case to capital letters ... 41
Writing words ... 42

A look back
What can you remember? ... 44
Self-assessment ... 48

Understanding, listening and speaking

Talking about things we need

⭐ Which things go together? Join them.
Say what you can do with each pair.

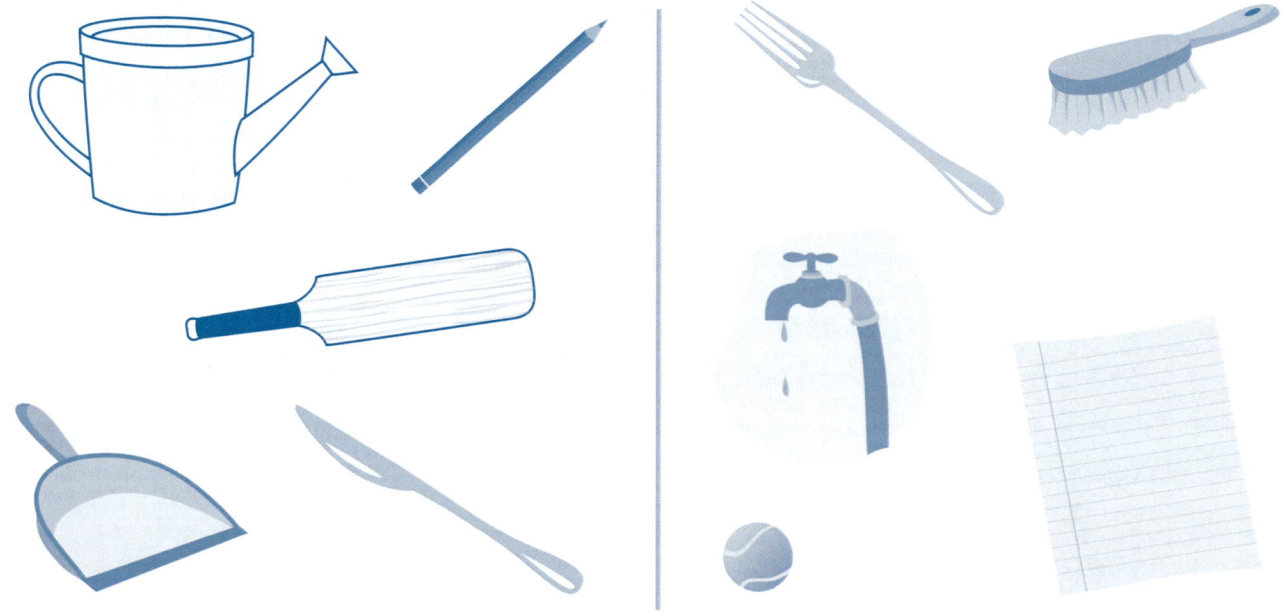

⭐ Tick the things you can cut with scissors.
Say the things you cannot cut.

Understanding, listening and speaking

⭐ What do you need to make the things in each box? Join them.

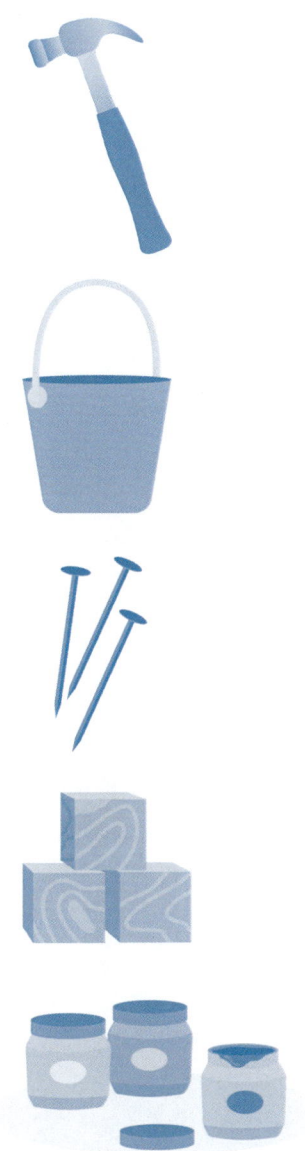

⭐ Talk about when you made something. What did you use?

⭐ Tick the things you can sweep up with a brush.
Say why you cannot sweep some of the things.

Understanding, listening and speaking

Questions and answers

To answer a question, look for clues in the picture.

To ask a question, use these **question words**:

| where | why | what | when | how |

 Answer the questions. Look for clues!

Why is she under a tree?

Where is she standing?

What are they doing?

How many children are running?

When do you play outside?

6

Understanding, listening and speaking

⭐ Now you ask some questions about the picture.
Use the **question words**.

7

Understanding, listening and speaking

Matching and describing things we can do

☆ Say what the children are doing. Use these words:

| cycling | swinging | jumping | kicking |

Join the pairs.

Understanding, listening and speaking

 Say the things you can **do**. Colour them red.
Say the things you can **make**. Colour them blue.

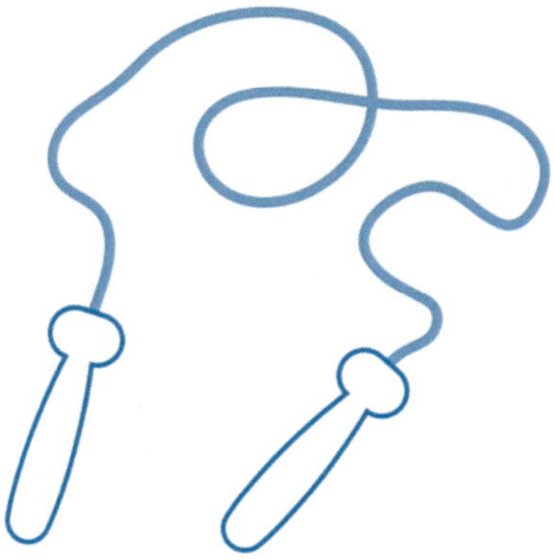

Exploring words

Word families: things I can do

⭐ Sing the rhyme.
Make actions for what you are doing.

This is the way we run in the sun,
Run in the sun,
Run in the sun.
This is the way we run in the sun
On a fun and sunny play day!

This is the way we hop in the sun,
Hop in the sun,
Hop in the sun.
This is the way we hop in the sun
On a fun and sunny play day!

This is the way we nap in the sun,
Nap in the sun,
Nap in the sun.
This is the way we nap in the sun
On a fun and sunny play day!

Exploring words

This is the way we sit in the sun,
Sit in the sun,
Sit in the sun.
This is the way we sit in the sun
On a fun and sunny play day!

This is the way we pick in the sun,
Pick in the sun,
Pick in the sun.
This is the way we pick in the sun
On a fun and sunny play day!

Exploring words

 Think about what you like to do. Tell a friend.

 Tick the things you like to do.

run

sing

dance

kick

read

swim

12

Exploring words

 Draw the things you like to do.

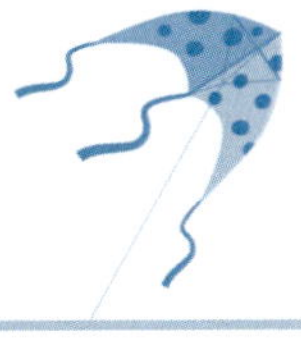

 Sing the rhyme on page 10 again with the things **you** like to do.

Exploring words

Repeating word patterns

 Sing this bit of the rhyme from page 10 again. Which words are repeating?

This is the way we run in the sun,

run in the sun, run in the sun.

This is the way we run in the sun
On a fun and sunny play day!

 How many times are these words repeating? Circle the number.

   1   2   3   4   5

run in the sun

14

Exploring words

 Sing it again. Which words are repeating?

This is the way we sit in the sun,

sit in the sun, sit in the sun.

This is the way we sit in the sun
On a fun and sunny play day!

 How many times are these words repeating? Circle the number.

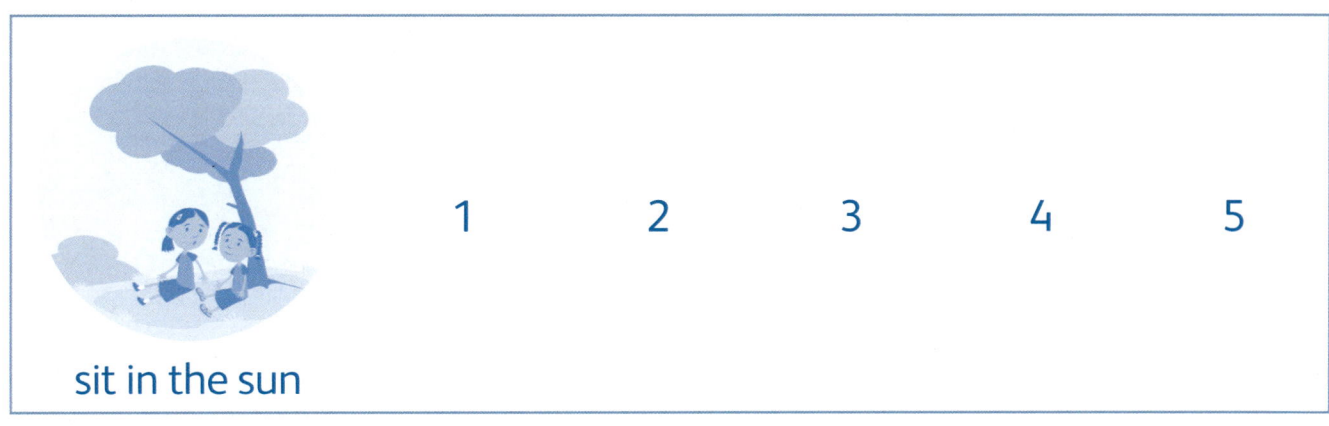

sit in the sun   1   2   3   4   5

Exploring words

Joining sentences with *and*

Use and to join two short sentences.

She likes skipping. She likes hopping.

She likes skipping **and** hopping.

⭐ Say two things the children are doing. Use the word **and**.

She is kicking **and** he is riding.

kicking

riding

building

and

pulling

jumping

skipping

16

Exploring words

 Draw and write what else you can do.

I can run **and** _____.

I can hop **and** _____.   I can kick **and** _____.

Tuning in to sounds and rhyme

Sounds all around us

⭐ Find the things on the map that make a sound.
Join each to its matching picture. Make the sounds.

Tuning in to sounds and rhyme

⭐ Add two more things to the map that make a sound.
Make the sounds.

19

Tuning in to sounds and rhyme

Make the sound!

⭐ Play the game *I hear with my little ear*.

It is a game for two players.

You will need:

counters   spinner

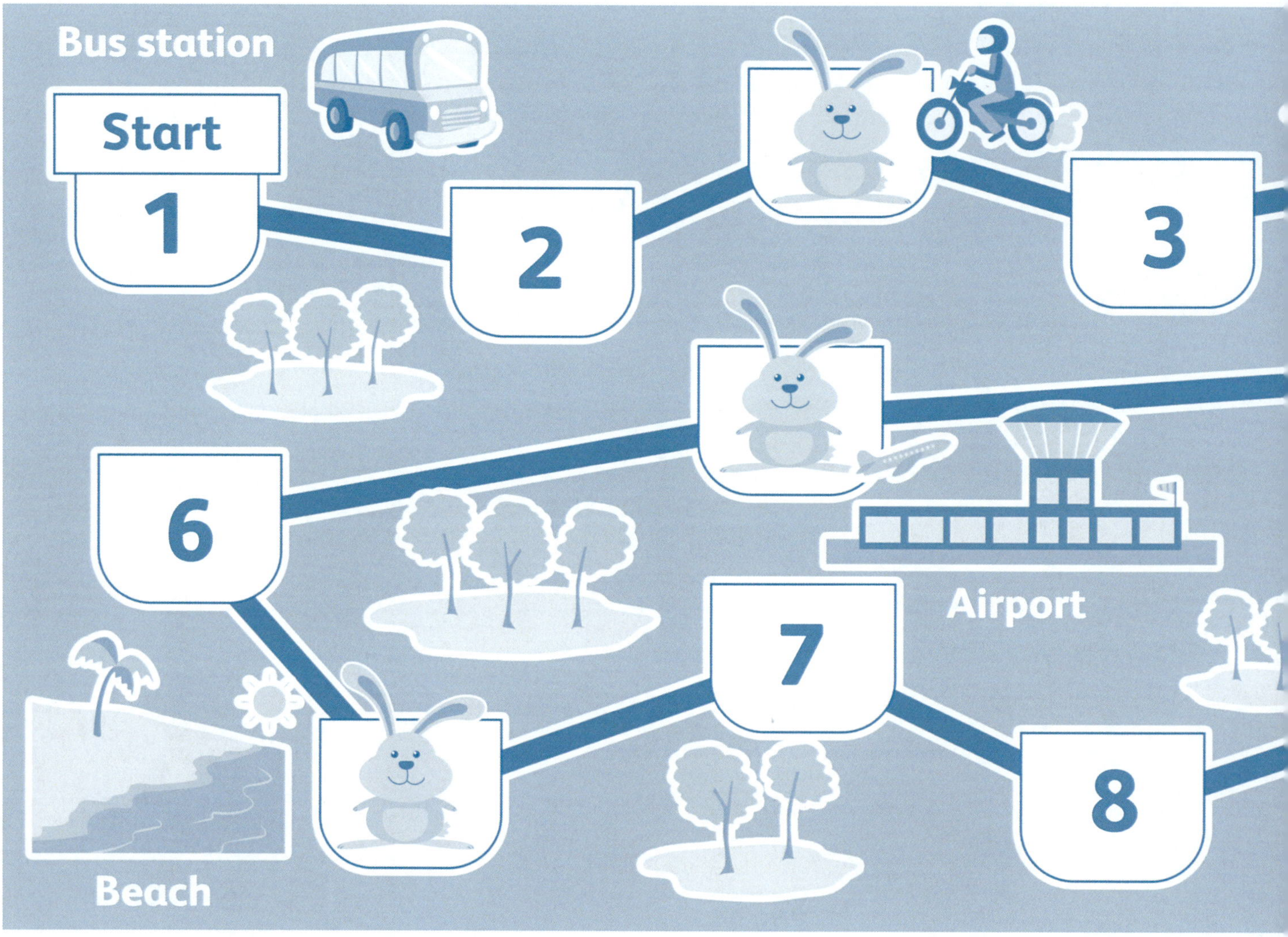

Bus station

Start
1
2
3
6
7
8

Airport

Beach

How to play:
- Start at the bus station.
- Take turns to spin the spinner. Move that number of spaces on the map.
- If you land on a 🐰 check where you are in the town. Choose something you might hear there and say:
I hear with my little ear a sound like this … and make that sound.

20

Tuning in to sounds and rhyme

I hear with my little ear a sound like this: *brrum, brrum, brrum …*

Is it the *brrum, brrum* of a car?

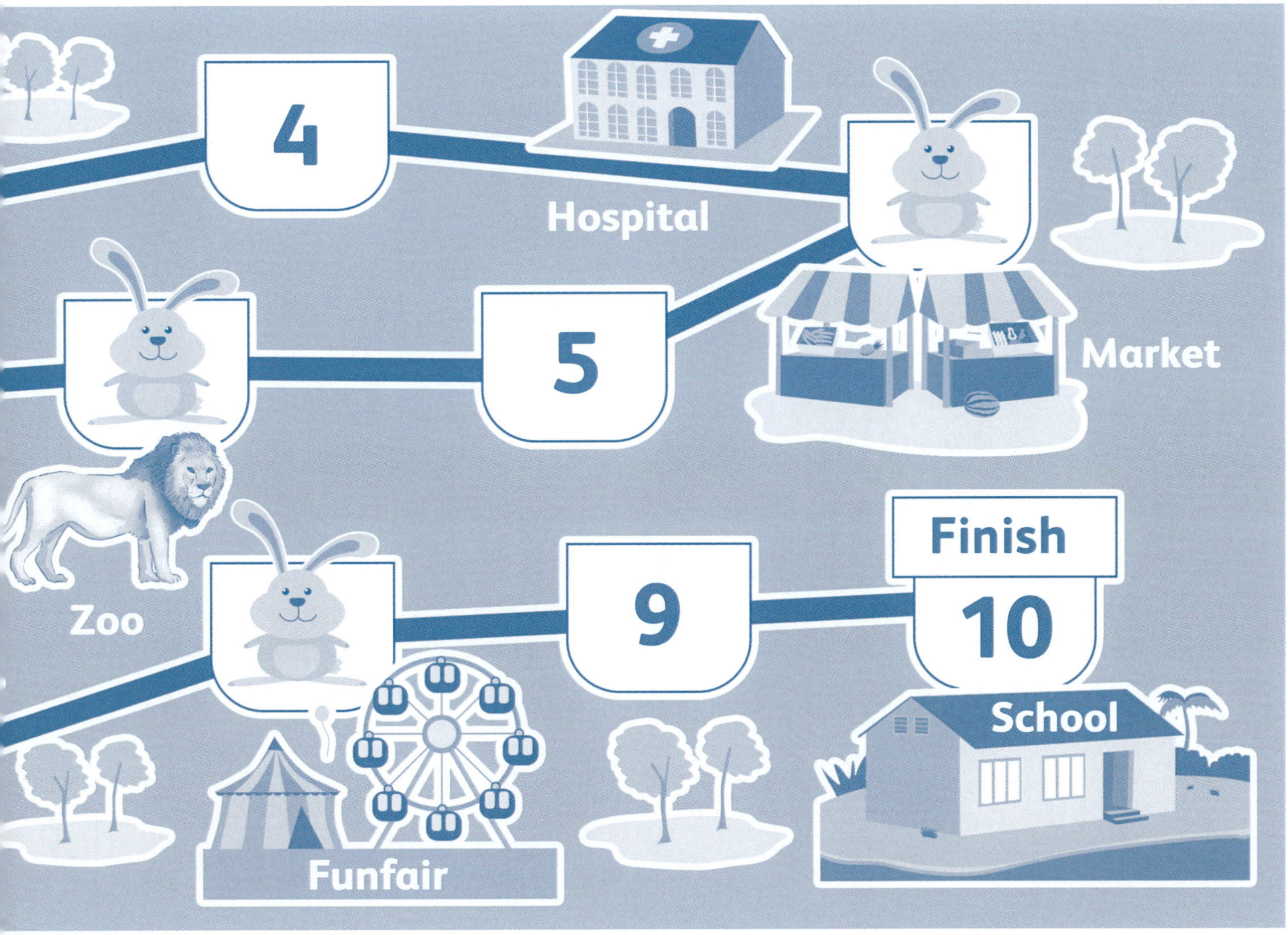

- The other player must guess what you are thinking of. Give them 3 guesses.
- If their guess is correct, then have another go. Spin again!
- If their guess is not correct, go back one space. Then it is their turn to spin.
- The winner is the first player to reach the school.

Tuning in to sounds and rhyme

Rhyming words

Rhyming words have some repeating letters with the same letter sounds.

cat and **hat** are rhyming words.

pen and **hen** are rhyming words.

⭐ Choose a rhyming word for each set. Write it and draw the picture.

rat   bug   rocks   pen

22

Tuning in to sounds and rhyme

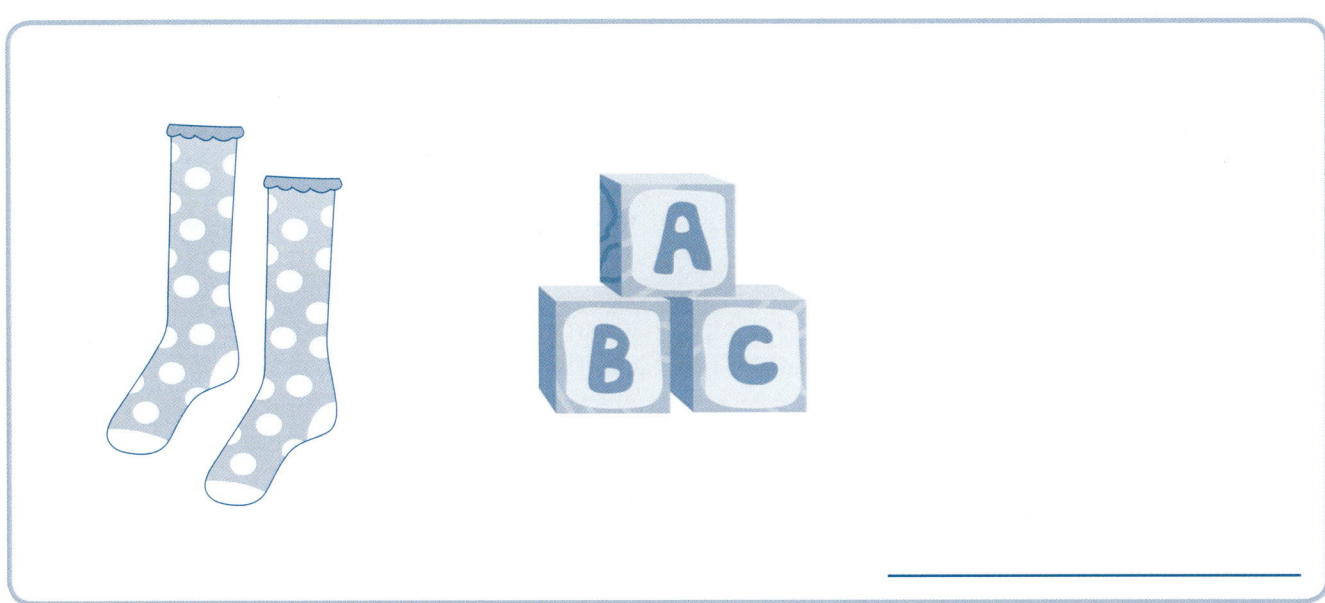

Tuning in to sounds and rhyme

 Name each picture. Find the rhyming pairs. Join them.

Tuning in to sounds and rhyme

 Read this rhyme. Draw a picture of the word that rhymes with each number in the box below.

 1, 2. Do up your shoe.
3, 4. Bang on the door.
5, 6. Pick up the bricks.
7, 8. Sit on the gate.
9, 10. A big fat hen!

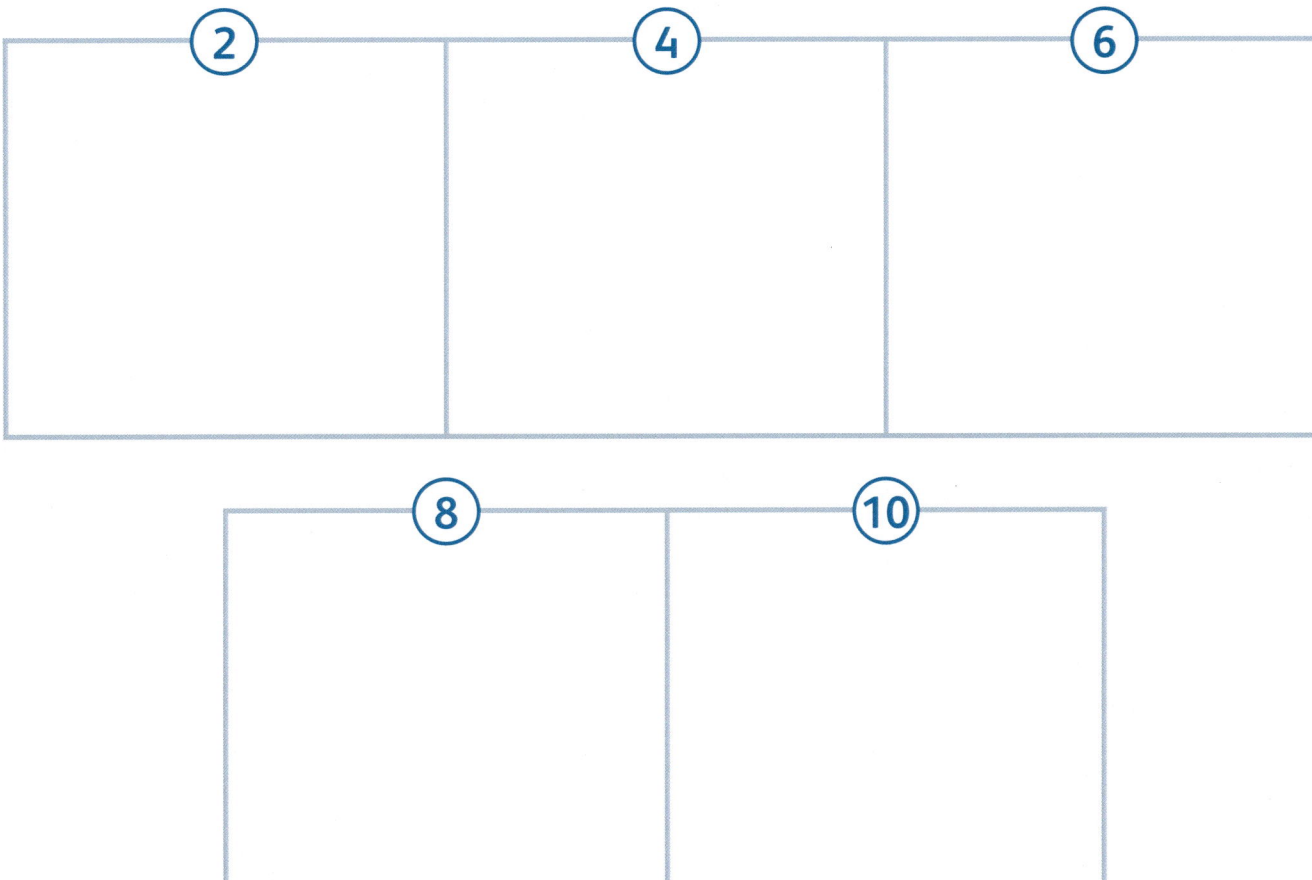

② ④ ⑥

⑧ ⑩

 Read this rhyme. Colour each pair of rhyming words the same colour.

I hear thunder!
Let's get under.
Pitter-patter rain-drops
Pitter-patter rain-plops
Has it stopped yet?
I'm all wet!

25

Letters and sounds 1

Matching letter sounds to letter shapes

☆ Say the word for each picture. Which letter sound begins the word? Circle the letter that begins the word.

f e   b g   c t

d g   a l   f t

☆ Say the word for each picture. Which letter sound ends the word? Circle the letter that ends the word.

t g   h m   t b

k f   g d   n p

26

Letters and sounds 1

Reading words

 Join each word to its picture.

map   cat   duck   bell   bed   mug

 Read and draw.

a sad man	a sock and a hat	a doll in a bed
a red bus	a cat on a rug	a fat duck

Letters and sounds 1

Writing letters

Say the word for each picture. Which letter sound begins the word? Write its letter.

28

Letters and sounds 1

⭐ Change a letter each time. Write the new word.

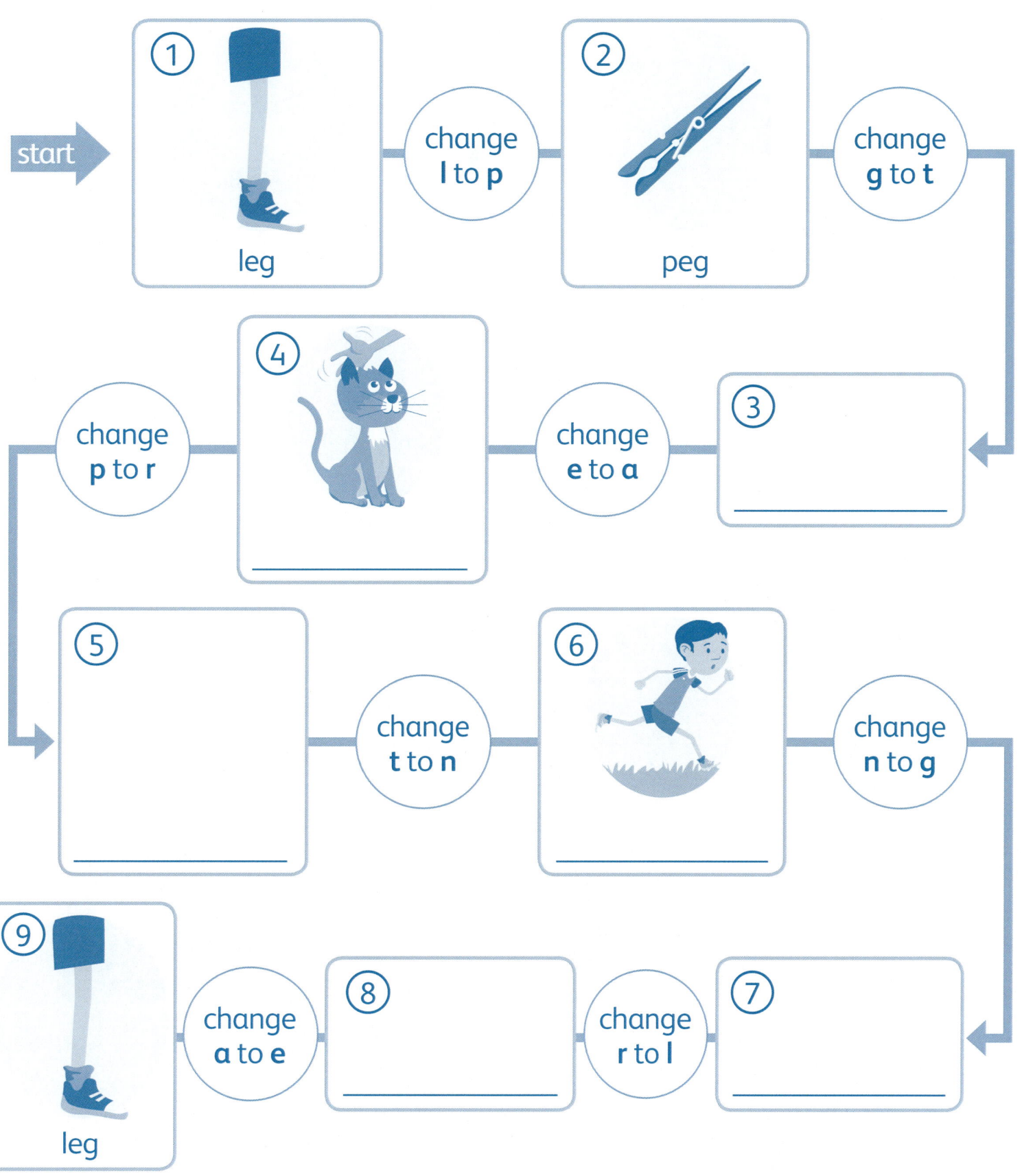

⭐ Draw the picture in box 5.

Reading real-life stories

Story characters

Story characters are people or animals in stories.

⭐ Talk about some story characters that you know. Tell a friend about them.

⭐ Say the names of these story characters. Talk about who they are in the family and what they look like.

I am Dad.

I am Gran or Ma Ma.

I am Grandad or Ye Ye.

I am Mum.

I am Lan.

Baby Lok

30

Reading real-life stories

 Read the descriptions. Join each to the correct picture.

Mum and Dad

Lok and Lan

Grandad and Gran

Lan on Dad

Lok in a cot

 Describe one of the characters to a friend. Can they guess who it is?

Reading real-life stories

Story settings

Story settings are places where stories happen.

 Where is Lan? Join each story book to its setting.

school   town   home

Reading real-life stories

 Where do you visit with your family? Draw the places you go in the box.

Reading real-life stories

Story events

Story events are the things that happen in stories.

⭐ Look at each story. Write 1, 2 or 3 in each box to show the order. Tell each story.

34

Reading real-life stories

Reading real-life stories

 Look at the pictures. Tell the story.

 Draw a time when you felt excited and then upset. Tell your story to a friend.

Reading real-life stories

 Look at the pictures. Find and join the correct story ending. Tell each story.

| Story A | Story B | Story C |

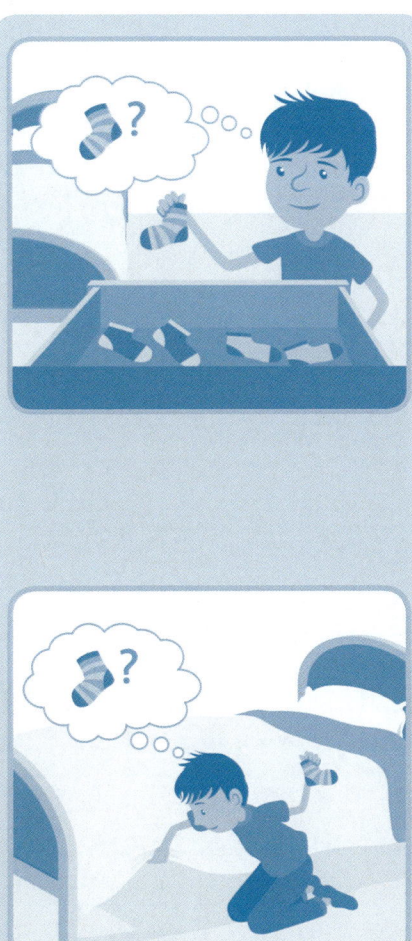

Writing

Writing patterns

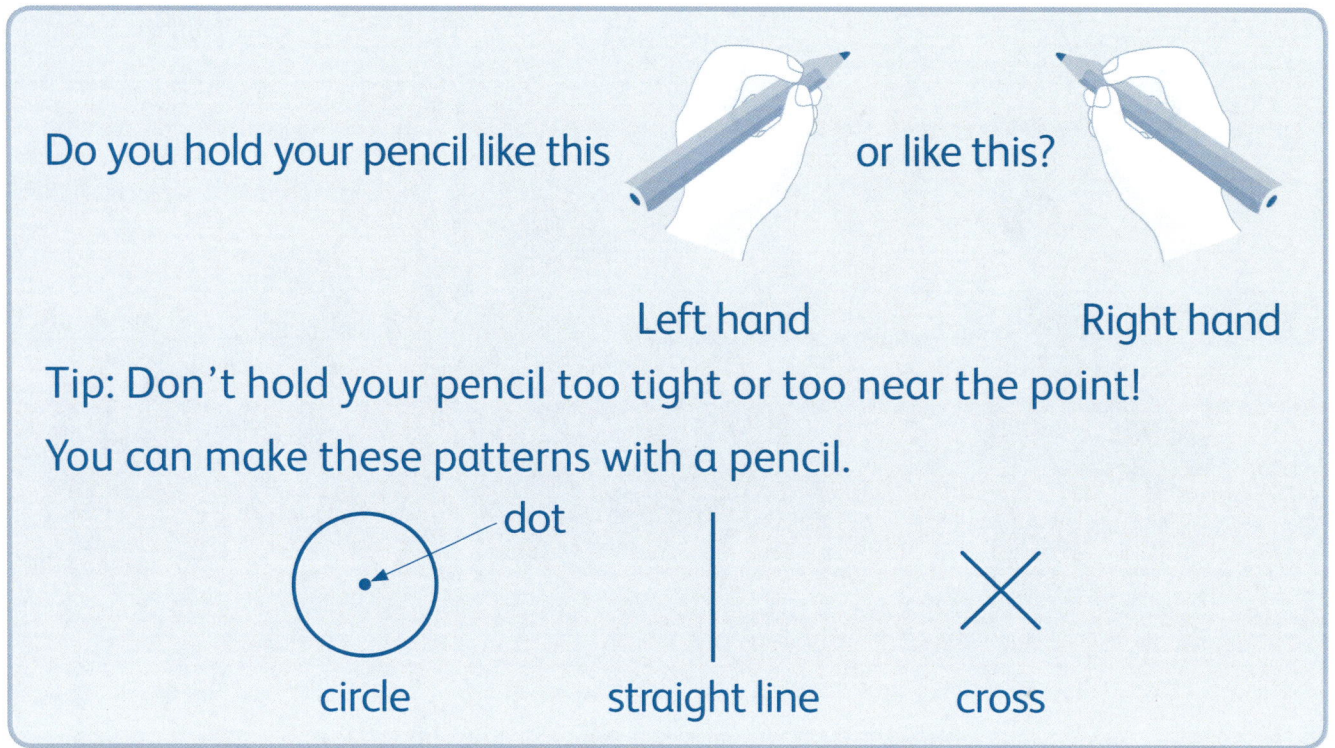

Do you hold your pencil like this   or like this?

Left hand   Right hand

Tip: Don't hold your pencil too tight or too near the point!

You can make these patterns with a pencil.

circle — dot   straight line   cross

⭐ What patterns can you see in the picture? Tell a friend.

⭐ Draw dots, straight lines and crosses on the plain things in the picture.

Writing

 Trace these patterns with your finger.
Then trace them with your pencil.

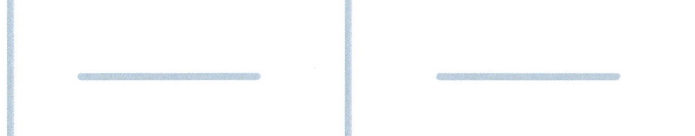 

 Put a dot in each circle. Which writing tool will you use to make the dot?

Writing

Matching letter shapes

☆ Join the matching letter pairs.

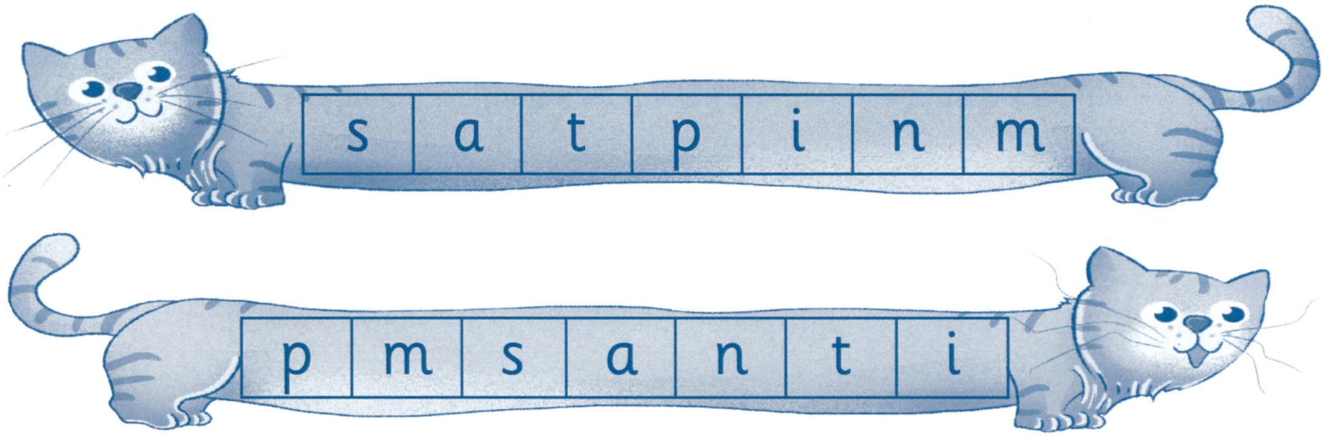

s a t p i n m

p m s a n t i

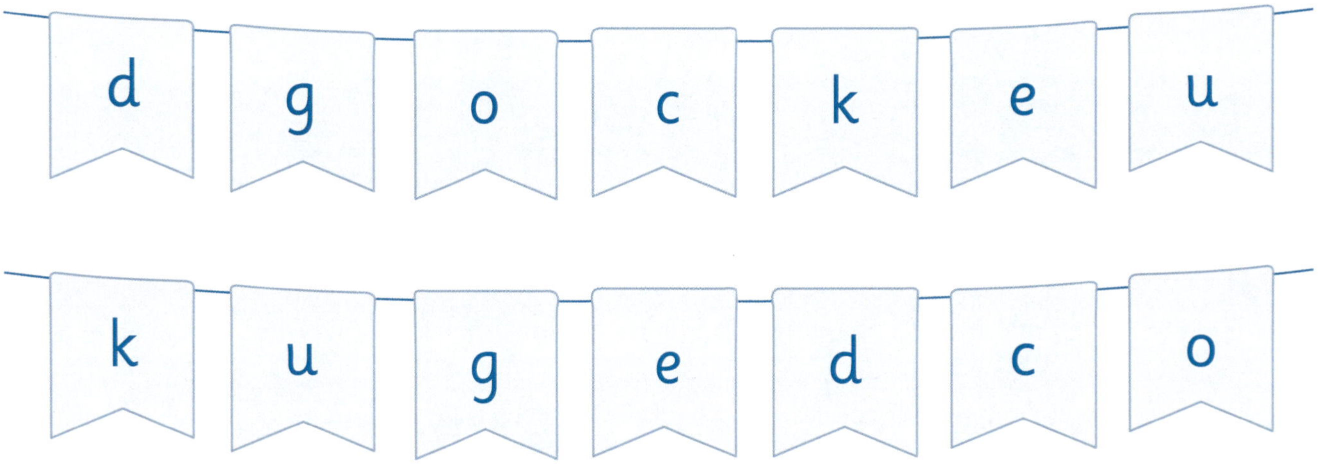

d g o c k e u

k u g e d c o

ck h b f l ss

b f l ss ck h

☆ Point to each letter or letters and say the sound.

Writing

Matching lower case to capital letters

All lower case letters have a partner capital letter.

A B C D E F G H I J K L M N O P Q R S T U V W X Y Z
a b c d e f g h i j k l m n o p q r s t u v w x y z

 Join each capital letter to its lower case letter partner.

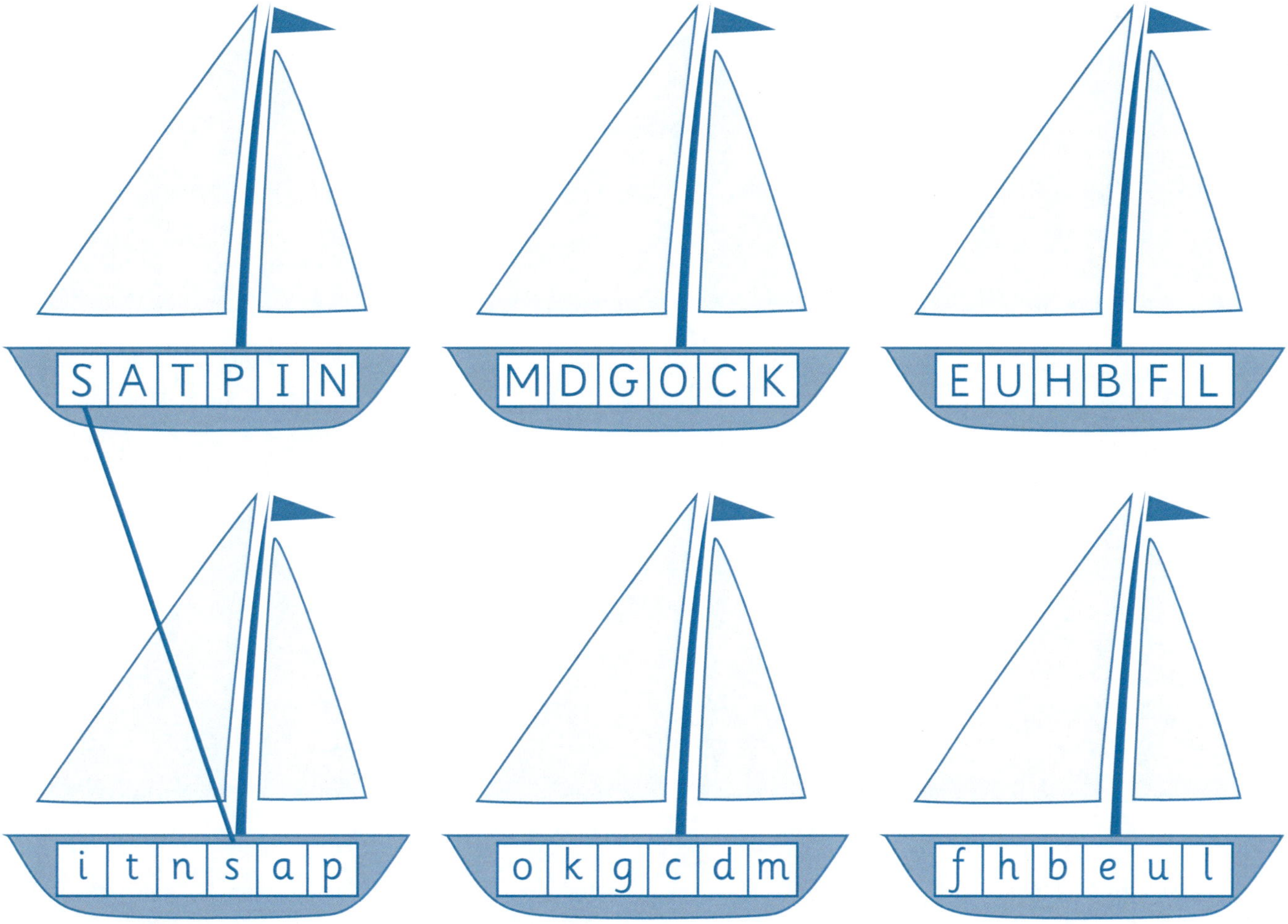

| S A T P I N | | M D G O C K | | E U H B F L |

| i t n s a p | | o k g c d m | | f h b e u l |

 Write your name here. Begin with a capital letter.

Writing

Writing words

⭐ Say the word for each picture. Write the letter(s) for each sound to make the word.

Writing

 Change a letter. Write the new word.

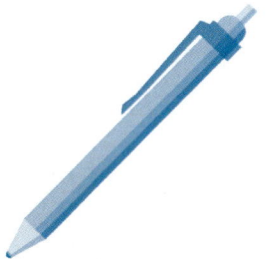

pen

Change p to t. _____

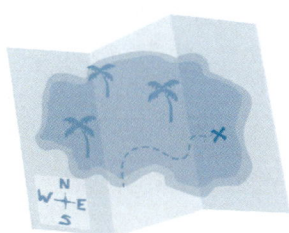

map

Change a to o. _____

doll

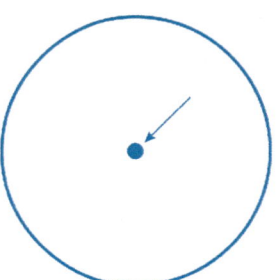

Change ll to t. _____

A look back

What can you remember?

★ Say what the children need. Join the pairs.

★ Describe each picture. Tick the pictures that show children doing things.

A look back

 Draw a picture of you doing things.
What are you doing?

 Join each number to the picture of the word that rhymes with it.

2   4   6   8   10

A look back

 Say a word for each picture. What letter sound is the same in each? Write the letter.

 Say the letter sound.
Draw two things in the box that begin with the letter sound.

s   f

A look back

 Join the matching lower case and capital letters to make the picture. Start at F.

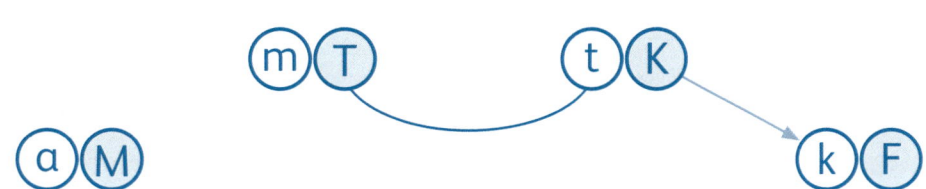

 Make a pattern on the T-shirt.
Use these patterns:

   —|

47

A look back

Self-assessment

Colour the stars to show what you can do!

Understanding, listening and speaking	I can name things and know what we use them for.	☆
	I can ask and answer questions.	☆
Exploring words	I can learn and use new words about things I do.	☆
	I can join in with repeating parts of rhymes.	☆
	I can link my sentences with the word *and*.	☆
Tuning in to sounds and rhyme	I can name and make the different sounds around me.	☆
	I can say simple rhymes and can match rhyming words.	☆
Letters and sounds 1	I can say the letter sound at the start and end of a word.	☆
	I can blend letter sounds to read simple words.	☆
	I can say a letter sound and write its matching letter shape.	☆
Reading real-life stories	I can describe and name story characters.	☆
	I can describe and name story settings.	☆
	I can describe what happens in a simple story and put it in the right order.	☆
Writing	I can copy and write patterns with dots, straight lines and crosses.	☆
	I can match lower case and capital letters.	☆
	I can write simple words and read them.	☆